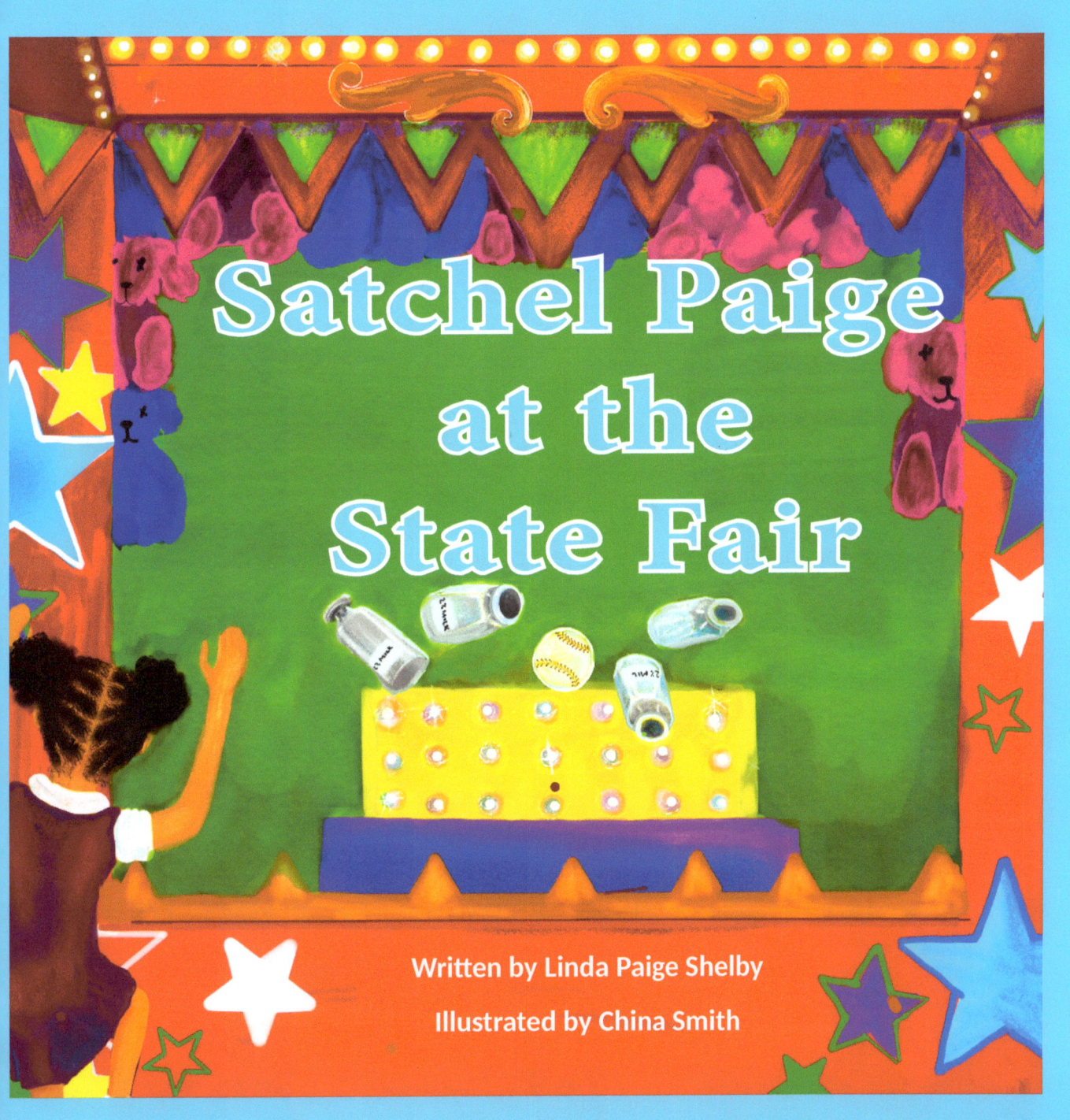

SATCHEL PAIGE AT THE STATE FAIR

By Linda Paige Shelby

Illustrated by China Smith

Copyright 2020 by Linda Paige Shelby

ALL RIGHTS RESERVED

No part of this publication may be reproduced, stored in a retrieval system, or transmitted, in any form or by any means--electronic, mechanical, photocopying, recording or otherwise--without prior written permission.

ISBN-13: 978-1-7330266-2-8

Published January 2020 by Personal Chapters LLC

Kansas City, MO 64114

personalchapters@gmail.com • www.personalchapters.com

ABOUT SATCHEL PAIGE

Leroy Robert "Satchel" Paige (July 7, 1906-June 8, 1982) was a Negro League Baseball and Major League Baseball (MLB) pitcher. He became one of the most famous and successful players from the Negro League. He played for several teams in the Negro League, including the Pittsburgh Crawfords and the Kansas City Monarchs. After signing with the Cleveland Indians, at age 42, he became the oldest rookie in Major League Baseball, helping the Indians win the World Series. He was inducted into the National Baseball Hall of Fame in 1971. On July 28, 2006, a statue of Satchel Paige was unveiled in Cooper Park, Cooperstown, New York, commemorating the contributions of the Negro Leagues to baseball.

It was late summer and time for the family trip to the Missouri State Fair in Sedalia, Missouri. Attending the fair was the highlight of the end of summer. We were filled with excitement. Because Dad traveled during baseball season, he couldn't go to the fair with us. This time it was going to be very special, because Dad was home and going to the fair.

That morning we woke up to the smell of bacon and cinnamon toast with scrambled eggs and grits that Mom was preparing for breakfast. She was also making her delicious, crispy fried chicken and potato salad to take along for lunch. We had cupcakes, fruit and bologna sandwiches to snack on. Dad's lemonade was on ice and there were bottles of soda pop for us kids. We always had plenty of good food to eat.

After breakfast Dad said, "Load 'em up, it's time to get on the road!" We began loading all the food, blankets and the cooler in the car. I was the first to call "window seat." When everyone was in the car we began our trip to the fair.

We sang and told "knock knock" jokes. All I thought about was the cotton candy, corn dogs, buttered popcorn and other delightful treats at the fair.

When we arrived, there were crowds of people all around. After Dad parked, we sprang from the car. "Stay together, I don't want anyone getting lost," Mom said.

It was exciting to see all the baby farm animals. Mom was going to buy fresh tomatoes, okra and green beans. Dad said he may buy a couple of baby chicks or a baby rabbit. We already had two cats, two dogs and a pet raccoon named Racky.

As we walked through the fairgrounds our first stop was for cotton candy and next, chocolate covered ice cream bars.

With our hands filled with good things to eat, we started walking toward the carnival games.

The first game we passed was the ring toss.

"Play this one, Daddy!" we said.

"Nope," he answered, as he kept walking.

Next, we passed the duck shooting game. We asked Dad, "Are you going to play this game?

"Nope," he said, as he continued walking.

We passed the basketball hoop game, but Dad kept walking.

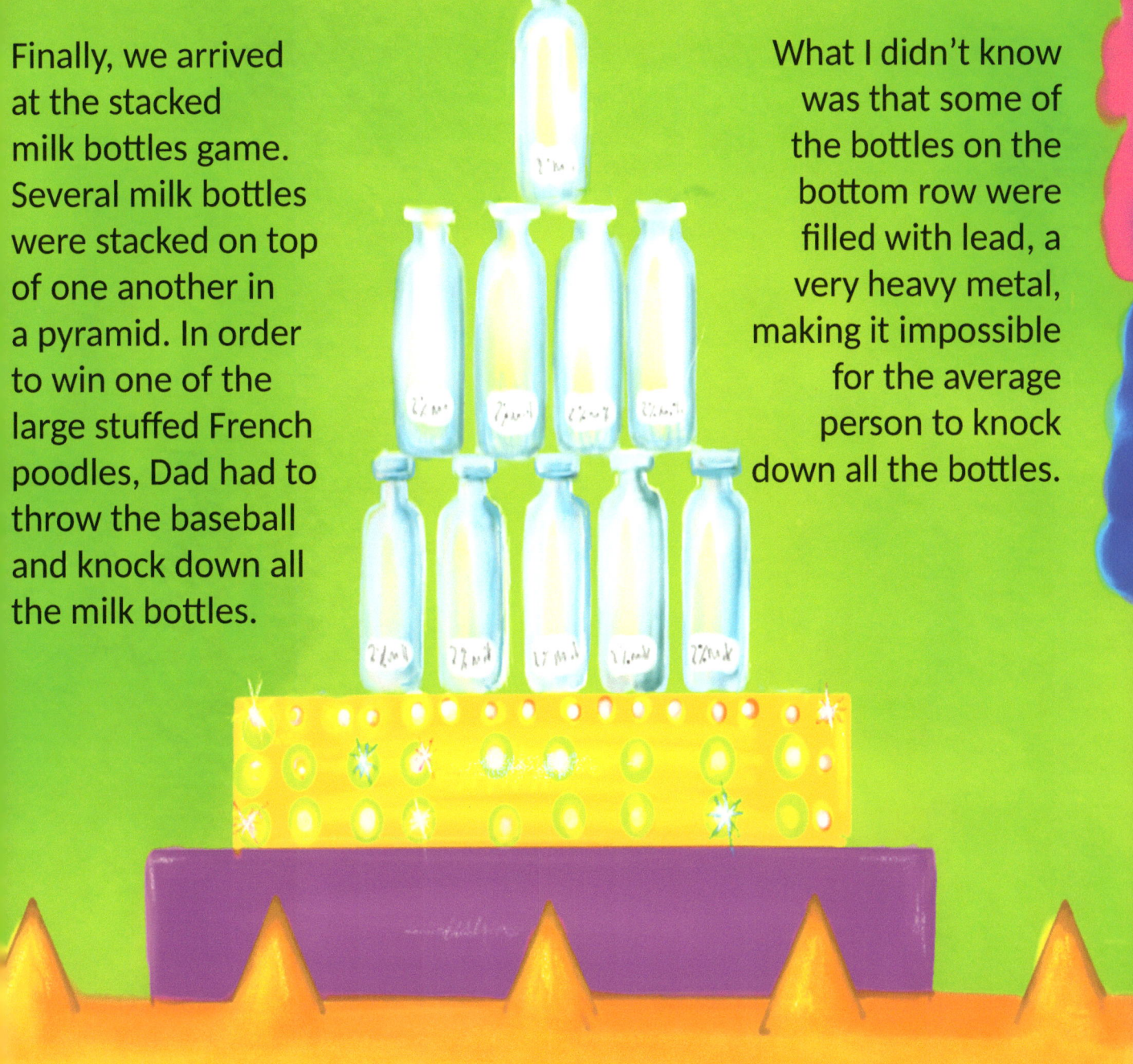

Finally, we arrived at the stacked milk bottles game. Several milk bottles were stacked on top of one another in a pyramid. In order to win one of the large stuffed French poodles, Dad had to throw the baseball and knock down all the milk bottles.

What I didn't know was that some of the bottles on the bottom row were filled with lead, a very heavy metal, making it impossible for the average person to knock down all the bottles.

Now it was Dad's turn. We stood on each side of him. Dad paid the attendant, who gave him three baseballs. Dad turned to his side and threw the balls.

W- H- A- M!

The milk bottles went flying off the table. The attendant looked surprised. We jumped up and down. "Yeah," we shouted. Dad knocked down all the milk bottles.

"Which stuffed animal do you want, Sir?" asked the attendant.

"The pink one," we shouted.

The attendant restacked the milk bottles.

Dad turned to his side and threw the baseball. W-H-A-M! All the milk bottles went flying off the table again. "Yeah!" we shouted. The attendant could not believe it.

"What color poodle do you want?" the attendant asked. "The blue one, the blue one," we shouted. Just then an older man who had been watching behind the counter said, "That's all, only two stuffed animals per customer." Dad was laughing so hard, he could barely speak. "Wait a minute."

"No sir, here's your money back. I've never seen anyone throw like that!" the older man said. Dad just smiled. Mom and Dad chuckled as we walked away.

We talked and talked about Dad knocking down all those milk bottles. He would have won all the toys in that booth. We thought our Dad was the most amazing father on the earth. We were so proud of our Dad and we wanted to make sure he knew it.

We never fogot that trip with Dad to the Missouri State Fair, and I'm sure those two men didn't either.

We also learned a valuable lesson Dad taught us ....

When obstacles are stacked against you,

throw as hard as you can!

LINDA PAIGE SHELBY, Author

Linda Paige Shelby is the daughter of the legendary baseball pitcher, Leroy "Satchel" Paige and his wife, Lahoma. Linda is one of eight siblings, born and raised in Kansas City, Missouri. Linda is a mother of four and a grandmother. She enjoys cooking and gardening.

CHINA SHELBY SMITH, Illustrator

China Shelby Smith is the daughter of Linda Shelby. China is married and mother of twin boys. She was born and raised in Detroit, Michigan. China was selected to participate in the DaimlerChrysler Art Program, attended Cass Technical High School and the Detroit Institute of Art. She is a graduate of the University of Michigan.

www.ingramcontent.com/pod-product-compliance
Lightning Source LLC
Chambersburg PA
CBHW041408160426
42811CB00103B/1551